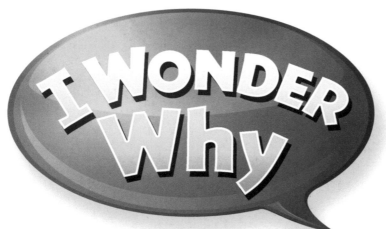

I WONDER Why

Leaves
Change Color
and other questions about plants

Andrew Charman

KINGFISHER

NEW YORK

KINGFISHER
LONDON & NEW YORK

Copyright © Kingfisher 2012
Published in the United States by Kingfisher,
175 Fifth Ave., New York, NY 10010
Kingfisher is an imprint of Macmillan
Children's Books, London.
First published 1997 by Kingfisher
This edition published 2012 by Kingfisher

Consultant: Michael Chinery

Distributed in the U.S. and Canada by Macmillan,
175 Fifth Ave., New York, NY 10010

Library of Congress Cataloging-in-Publication data
has been applied for.

ISBN 978-0-7534-6698-8 (HC)
ISBN: 978-0-7534-6697-1 (PB)

Kingfisher books are available for special promotions and
premiums. For details contact: Special Markets Department,
Macmillan, 175 Fifth Avenue, New York, NY 10010.

For more information, please visit www.kingfisherbooks.com

Printed in China
9 8 7 6 5 4 3 2 1
1TR/1011/WKT/UG/140MA

Illustrations: Andrew Beckett (Garden Studio) 6–7; Peter
Dennis (Linda Rogers) 28–29; Richard Draper 14–15; Chris
Forsey cover, 8bm, 12–13, 30–31; Biz Hull (Artist Partners)
8–9; Ian Jackson 4–5, 16–17, 20–21, 26–27; Tony Kenyon
(B. L. Kearley) all cartoons; Nicki Palin 10–11, 24–25;
Dan Wright 18–19, 22–23.

CONTENTS

4 What is a plant?

4 Where do plants grow?

5 Are plants really alive?

6 Why do trees have leaves?

6 Why do some trees lose their
 leaves in the fall?

7 Why do leaves change color?

8 Why do roots grow so long?

9 Why are stems so straight?

10 Which plants grow in water?

10 Which are the smallest plants?

11 Which forests grow in the ocean?

12 Which plant . . . traps a treat?

13 . . . fools a fly?

13 . . . snares a snack?

14 Why do plants have flowers?

15 Which flower fools a bee?

15 Which is the smelliest flower?

16 Why is fruit so sweet and juicy?

16 Which plant shoots from the hip?

17 Which seeds sail away?

17 Which fruit gets forgotten?

18 When does a seed begin to grow?

18 Do all plants grow from seeds?

19 Which plant grows the fastest?

20 Are fungi plants?

20 What puffs out of a puffball?

21 Which are the oldest plants?

22 Why do trees have thorns?

23 Why do stinging nettles sting?

23 Which plants look like pebbles?

24 Which plants hitch a ride to the light?

24 Which plant has a private pool?

25 Which plants strangle and squeeze?

26 Can plants grow in a desert?

27 Can you pick fruit in the desert?

27 Can you find flowers in the desert?

28 Which are the tastiest plants?

28 Why do carrot plants grow carrots?

29 Do people ever eat grass?

30 What are old plants good for?

31 What are plants good for today?

32 Index

What is a plant?

Plants are living things. They come in all shapes and sizes, from tiny waterweeds to towering trees. Plants are different from animals in one very important way—they can make food for themselves from sunlight. Animals can't do this. They depend on plants for their food.

Where do plants grow?

There are about 400,000 different kinds of plants on Earth, and they grow just about everywhere—fields and forests, deserts and mountains. Besides air, the two things plants need are sunlight and water, so you won't find them in places that are completely dark or dry.

All of the food in the world starts with plants. You may eat eggs, meat, and cheese, but without plants, no chicken or cow could produce these foods!

Are plants really alive?

Plants are just as alive as you are. They need air, food, and water to grow, and they can make many new plants like themselves. This proves that they are alive. Things such as stones and rocks don't feed, grow, or have young because they are not alive.

Corals and sea anemones may look like plants, but they are imposters. In fact, they are animals!

Why do trees have leaves?

Like all plants, trees need their leaves in order to stay alive. Leaves are a tree's food factories. They contain sticky green stuff called chlorophyll. The chlorophyll uses water, sunlight, and carbon dioxide in the air to make a sugary food. The food is then carried to every part of the tree in a sweet and sticky juice called sap.

If you have ever chewed a blade of grass, you will know how sweet sap tastes. Hungry young caterpillars think so, too. That's why they eat leaves!

Why do some trees lose their leaves in the fall?

Big green leaves are useful in the spring and summer. They make food while the Sun shines and the days are long. When the days get shorter, there's less time for making food and a tree must live off its food reserves. Rather than feed their leaves, too, some trees shed their leaves in the fall.

The way that plants make food in their leaves is called photosynthesis. During photosynthesis, plants take in carbon dioxide from the air. And they give out oxygen—the gas we all need in order to survive.

We call plants that lose their leaves in the fall deciduous. Evergreens have tough leaves that can survive the winter. Evergreens still lose their leaves but not all at the same time.

Why do leaves change color?

It's the chlorophyll in a plant's leaves that makes them look green. But in the fall, the chlorophyll breaks down. Once the green coloring is gone, the leaves' other colors show through—beautiful shades of red, yellow, and gold.

Why do roots grow so long?

Long roots fix a plant firmly in the ground so that it won't fall over on windy days. But roots do another job, too. By spreading out far and wide, they can suck up water and nutrients from the soil around. Then the roots send the water up the stem or trunk and into the leaves.

In the strongest winds, a tree can sometimes be blown right over. Its roots are wrenched out of the ground as the tree falls down with a crash.

A wild fig tree in South Africa grew roots 400 feet (120m) down into the soil. If it were put on the roof of a 40-story office building, its roots would reach down to the ground.

At the ends of the roots are tiny hairs that burrow into the spaces between the clumps of soil.

Sunflowers not only grow up toward the light, but their flowers follow the Sun! As the Sun appears to move across the sky throughout the day, the flower heads turn to face it.

Why are stems so straight?

A plant needs to hold its leaves up to the sunshine, which it uses to make its food. Many plants grow tall, straight stems so that they can beat their neighbors to the sunlight.

Not all plants have straight stems. Some have stems that bend and curl, clambering their way over nearby plants as they climb up to the light.

Which plants grow in water?

The giant water lily grows in the lakes and rivers of South America. Its roots lie deep in the mud, and its huge leaves float on the water's surface. This is the best place for catching the sun! Each leaf curls up at the rim so that it can push other leaves aside.

The giant water lily's leaves grow on long, strong stems. On the underside of each leaf is a web of supporting veins. This makes the leaves so strong that a toddler could sit on one without sinking!

Which are the smallest plants?

Although some types of algae grow to be enormous plants, there are other algae so small that you can see them only through a microscope. The very smallest float in lakes and oceans and are called phytoplankton. They are so tiny that whales catch millions in every gulp!

The leaves and roots of water plants give food and shelter to many animals. But they are also places where hunters can hide.

Which forests grow in the ocean?

Huge forests of kelp grow off the coast of California in the United States. Kelp is a type of seaweed that grips onto rocks and sends long, ribbonlike stems up through the water. Some of the stems can be 660 feet (200m) long—as long as eight swimming pools laid end to end.

Not all water plants are rooted in the mud. Some seaweeds float in the water, thanks to pockets of air in their leaves—a lot like having their very own life preservers!

Which plant . . . traps a treat?

When an insect lands on a Venus flytrap, it gets a nasty surprise! It only has to brush against one tiny hair on an open leaf tip to make the leaf snap tightly shut. There's no escape for the poor insect. The flytrap changes it into a tasty soup that the plant slowly soaks up.

The bladderwort is an underwater meat eater. Along its leaves are bubble-shaped bags that suck in tiny creatures as they paddle past.

Did you know that flytraps can count? The first time an insect touches a hair on one of the leaf tips, the trap stays open. But if it touches it a second time, the trap snaps shut!

. . . fools a fly?

Pitcher plants have unusual vase-shaped leaves that tempt insects with a sweet smell. But the leaves are slippery traps. When a fly lands on one, it loses its footing, slips inside the "vase," and drowns in a pool of juice.

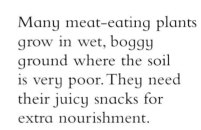

Many meat-eating plants grow in wet, boggy ground where the soil is very poor. They need their juicy snacks for extra nourishment.

. . . snares a snack?

The sundew's leaves are covered in hairs that sparkle with gluelike drops. When an insect lands on a leaf, it gets stuck fast. The more it struggles, the more it sticks. At last, the leaf folds over, traps the fly, and starts dissolving it into liquid food that the plant can drink up.

Why do plants have flowers?

Many plants have colorful, perfumed flowers that attract insects and other animals. The visitors feed on drops of sweet nectar inside the flowers. As they feed, they pick up a fine yellow dust called pollen that they carry to another flower. When the pollen rubs off on the second flower, that flower can start to make seeds.

This plant is called hot lips—and no wonder! The lipstick-red markings on its leaves are a wonderful way to attract visitors to its tiny flower.

Many trees and grasses spread their pollen in the wind. They don't need animal visitors, so they don't grow bright flowers.

14

Pollinators, such as this bat, don't mean to get pollen all over themselves. But a cactus flower is shaped in such a way that the bat just can't help it!

Which flower fools a bee?

A bee orchid's flowers look and smell just like female bees. Male bees zoom to the flowers, wanting to mate with them—but they have been tricked! The plant's just using them as mail carriers to deliver small packages of pollen to other orchids nearby.

During the summer, the air can be so full of pollen that it makes many people sneeze. Poor things—they haven't caught a cold; they have hay fever.

Which is the smelliest flower?

The dead-horse arum is well named—it smells like rotten meat! But blowflies love it. These plump flies usually lay their eggs inside the rotting bodies of dead animals. They are fooled by the plant's rotten smell and crawl inside it to lay their eggs, picking up pollen on the way.

Why is fruit so sweet and juicy?

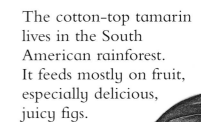

Plants make sweet, juicy fruit so that animals will eat them. Inside every fruit is one or more seeds. When an animal swallows the fruit, it swallows the seeds, too. These pass through its body and fall out in its droppings. In such good soil, the seeds soon start to grow into new plants!

You often see seeds floating through the air. Dandelion seeds grow their own fluffy parachutes. And sycamore seeds have wings that spin them to the ground like tiny helicopters.

Which plant shoots from the hip?

The Mediterranean squirting cucumber has a special way of spreading its seeds. As the fruit grows, it fills with a slimy juice. Day by day, the fruit grows fuller and fuller until it bursts, flinging the seeds far out into the air.

Which seeds sail away?

Coconut palms grow near the ocean, so the ripe coconuts often fall into the water. Protected by their hard shells, they float out to sea. After several weeks or months, they are washed up onto a beach, where they sprout and start to grow.

Fruit comes in many different colors, but most animals seem to like red fruit the best!

Which fruit gets forgotten?

Many animals feed on acorns, the fruit of the oak tree. Squirrels enjoy them so much that, every fall, they bury some in the ground as a snack for when food is short in the winter. The trouble is, the animals often forget where they have hidden their supply, so when the spring comes, young oaks start to grow.

When does a seed begin to grow?

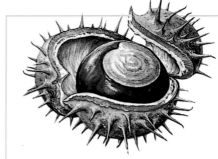

Inside every seed is the tiny beginning of a new plant. It starts to grow when the soil around the seed is warm and damp. At first, the baby plant feeds on a supply of food inside the seed. But as soon as its first leaves open, it begins to make food for itself.

The seed of the horse-chestnut tree has a tough brown coat. The coat rots away in the winter, and the young plant bursts through in the spring.

1. The bean seed swells with water and splits open. A root starts to grow.

2. Tiny hairs grow out from the branches of the root.

3. A shoot appears. It grows up toward the light.

Do all plants grow from seeds?

Strawberry plants don't need seeds to produce new plants. They can send out side shoots called runners. Where these touch the ground, roots begin to grow— then leaves and stems. In only a few weeks, there's a brand-new plant!

The coco-de-mer palm tree grows the largest seeds. They weigh 45 pounds (20kg)—as much as a big bag of potatoes.

Which plant grows the fastest?

The bamboo plant is the fastest-growing plant in the world. Some types can grow almost 3 feet (1m) a day. At that rate, they would reach the roof of a two-story house in a single week!

4. The shoot grows leaves. Now the new bean plant can make food for itself.

A cycad tree in Mexico must hold the record as the world's slowest-growing plant. After 120 years, it was only 4 inches (10cm) high!

Are fungi plants?

Fungi aren't really plants at all. They look like plants, and they grow in the same sort of places. But, unlike plants, they don't have leaves, stems, or roots, and they don't make their food from sunlight. A fungus grows by soaking up food from dead animals and plants.

What puffs out of a puffball?

A puffball is a kind of fungus that looks like a large, creamy ball. If you hit a ripe one, a cloud of dust puffs out of the top. This dust is actually millions of tiny specks called spores. Spores do the same job as seeds. If they land in rich soil, they will grow into brand-new puffballs.

Scientists have found more than 100,000 different types of fungi—and there are probably thousands more. The tiny, bright blue toadstools shown here grow in New Zealand.

Which are the oldest plants?

Soft mosses and tall ferns first appeared on land about 350 million years ago. But the very first plants appeared on Earth more than three billion years earlier. They were tiny microscopic plants called algae that floated in the ocean.

There were plants on land long before there were animals. Some of the kinds that plant-eating dinosaurs ate are still around today.

Did you know that the blue strands in some cheeses are a kind of fungus?

One kind of fungus not only feeds on dead animals—it kills them first! The tiny spores grow inside live ants, feeding on the juicy parts of their bodies. Soon, nothing is left but an ant's dry skeleton, with the toadstools growing out of it.

Why do trees have thorns?

Trees such as the acacia have thorns to keep plant-eating animals away, but they don't always work. Goats, camels, and giraffes, for example, have tough lips and mouths and long, curling tongues to get around the thorns. The plants will have to come up with another trick!

The leaves on the lowest branches of a holly tree are the prickliest, to keep animals from nibbling them. Higher up, the leaves are out of reach, so they are a lot less spiny.

Why do stinging nettles sting?

Stinging is another way plants protect themselves. Each leaf on a nettle is covered with small hairs as sharp as glass. If an animal sniffs one, the hair pricks the animal's nose and injects a drop of painful poison—ouch! It won't stick around to eat that leaf!

Milkweed is a poisonous plant, but the caterpillars of the monarch butterfly eat it and come to no harm. It even makes the caterpillars poisonous—so they don't get eaten by birds.

Which plants look like pebbles?

Pebble plants grow in the desert of southern Africa. Each one has two fat, juicy leaves that any animal would love to eat. But the plant protects itself by blending in with the background. Its leaves are disguised to look so pebblelike that animals pass it by.

23

Which plants hitch a ride to the light?

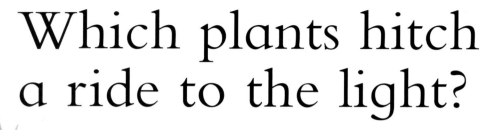

In rainforests, the tallest trees spread out their branches in the sunshine, making it shady down below. Because of this, some smaller plants don't get enough light. A group of plants called epiphytes have solved the problem by perching high up on the branches of trees and growing up there instead.

Which plant has a private pool?

Bromeliads are epiphytes that grow high up on rainforest trees. They don't use roots to collect water—every time it rains, the plants catch drops of water in a pool in the middle of their leaves. The tiny pools are perfect for tree frogs to relax in, too!

It's so wet in a rainforest that many plants have leaves with downward-pointing tips. They are like drainpipes for the rain to run down.

Lianas are climbing plants that dangle from rainforest trees. Some animals use them as ropes and swing on them through the trees.

Not all epiphytes collect water in their leaves. Some, such as orchids, have long, trailing roots that soak up water from the steamy air like a sponge.

Which plants strangle and squeeze?

The strangler fig is well named because it strangles other trees to death! Its seed sprouts high up on the branch of a tree. Week by week, its roots grow longer—wrapping around the branches, down the trunk, and into the ground. The fig then sucks all of the nutrients out of the soil, starving its host until it dies.

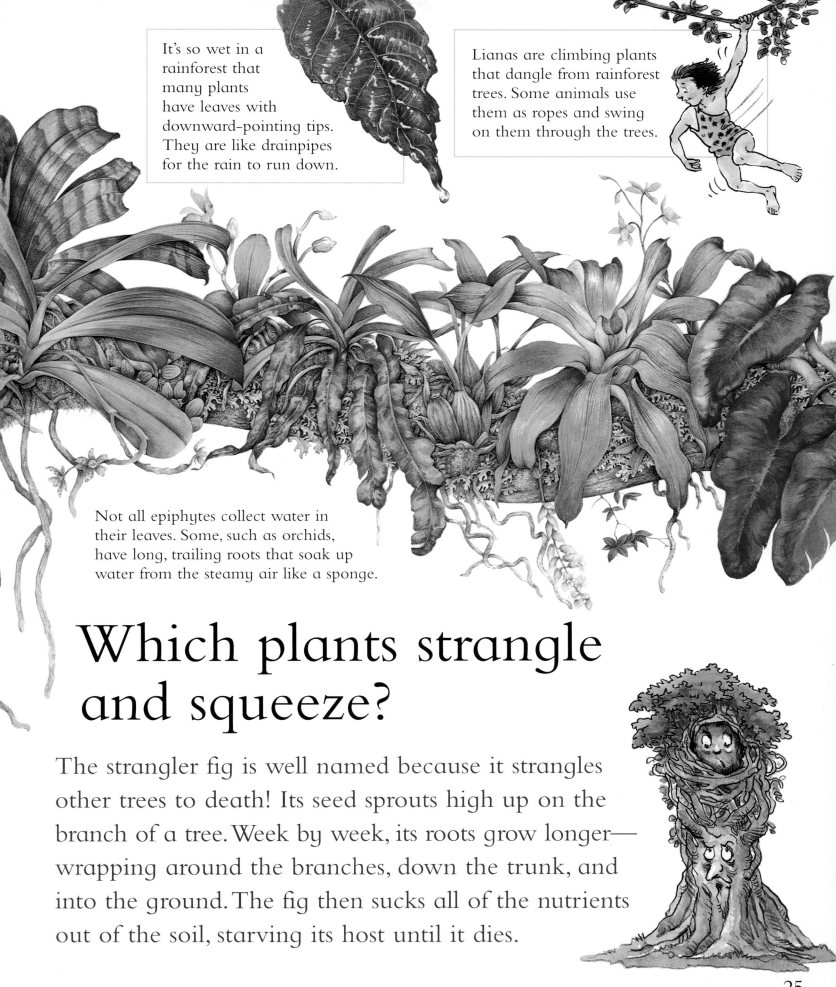

Can plants grow in a desert?

Plants can grow in a desert, but they need special ways to survive. Cacti have spreading roots that slurp up any rain as soon as it falls. Then they take great care of the water, storing it inside their fat, juicy stems. It may have to last them weeks, months, or even years.

Desert plants save lives! Many thirsty travelers have sucked lifesaving water from the juicy flesh of a cactus.

Can you pick fruit in the desert?

Huge bunches of sweet, sticky dates dangle from palm trees beside springs in the deserts of Africa and the Middle East. People have been picking the delicious fruit in these areas for more than 5,000 years.

A gila woodpecker makes a cool nest for itself by carving out a hole in a cactus. When it leaves, there's a long line of other birds who would like to move in!

Can you find flowers in the desert?

Daisies, poppies, and many other plants flower in the desert. The plants wither and die during the hot, dry months, but their seeds survive in the ground. When it rains, they soon spring into action. They grow into new plants and cover the dry desert with a beautiful carpet of flowers within a few weeks.

Which are the tastiest plants?

Most spices come from plants that grow in tropical parts of the world. For hundreds of years, merchants have traveled around the world to buy spices at markets like this.

Spices are made from plants. They have such a strong smell and taste that we use them in cooking to give food a kick. After being harvested, most spices are dried and then crushed to a powder that you can add to your food.

Spices are made from different parts of plants. Pepper comes from berries, cinnamon from bark, and ginger from a root.

Why do carrot plants grow carrots?

A carrot is a tasty food—but it's not really meant for us! Carrot plants live for only two years. In the first year, they make food that they store in a fat orange root. They use up the food in the second year while they are growing flowers and seeds—as long as the carrots haven't already been dug up!

Roots, berries, leaves, and seeds—plants give us so many wonderful foods that some people eat no animal foods at all. They are called vegans.

Do people ever eat grass?

Wheat, rice, corn, barley, oats, and rye are just some of the grasses that people eat all over the world. We don't eat the leaves like cows and other animals do.

We harvest the seeds. Then we either eat them whole or grind them into flour to make pasta, bread, and other important foods.

Scientists can improve seeds so that they grow into stronger, healthier plants. This helps farmers grow bigger and better crops.

What are old plants good for?

The coal we burn today comes from plants that grew even before there were dinosaurs!

Three hundred million years ago, there were huge forests of trees and ferns. As the plants died, they fell into swamps and were buried in the mud. Slowly, over millions of years, the plants were pressed down and turned into a black rock called coal. Coal is a fuel that we burn to make energy.

Shampoos, perfumes, and bath oils all include ingredients made from sweet-smelling plants. That's why you smell so sweet!

In some parts of the world, people run their cars on fuels made from corn, potato, and sugar-cane plants.

30

The corks that seal bottles of wine are made from the bark of the cork oak tree.

Many of the medicines we buy at a drugstore are made from plants.

All sorts of useful things are made from rubber. It comes from the sticky juice of the rubber tree.

What are plants good for today?

Today's plants are still giving us the food and oxygen we need to survive. They also help us make many useful things, such as paper, clothes, and medicines. Every year, scientists discover new plants and new ways to use them. So let's protect our plants.

Cotton

Flax

Cotton cloth is made from the soft hairs that surround the cotton plant's seeds. Linen is made from the stems of the flax plant.

Index

A

acacias 22
acorns 17
algae 10, 21

B

bamboo plants 19
bee orchids 15
bladderworts 12
bromeliads 24

C

cacti 15, 26, 27
carrots 28
chlorophyll 6, 7
cloth 31
coal 30
coco-de-mer palms 19
coconut palms 17
cork 31
cycads 19

D

dandelions 16
date palms 27
dead-horse arums 15
deciduous plants 7
deserts 4, 23, 26–27

E

epiphytes 24, 25
evergreens 7

F

ferns 21, 30
figs 8, 16, 25
flowers 9, 14–15, 27, 28
food (from plants) 4, 5,
   28–29, 31
fruit 16–17, 27
fungi 20, 21

G

grasses 6, 14, 29

H

hay fever 15
holly 22
horse chestnuts 18
hot lips 14

K

kelp 11

L

leaves 6–7, 8, 9, 10, 11,
   12, 13, 14, 18, 19, 22,
   23, 24, 25, 29
lianas 25

M

meat-eating plants 12–13
medicines 31
milkweeds 23
mosses 21

N

nectar 14
nettles 23

O

oaks 17
orchids 15, 25

P

paper 31
pebble plants 23
photosynthesis 6, 7
phytoplankton 10
pitcher plants 13
pollen 14, 15
puffballs 20

R

rainforests 16, 24–25
roots 8, 10, 11, 18, 20,
   24, 25, 26, 28, 29
rubber 31

S

sap 6, 31
seaweed 11
seeds 14, 16–17, 18–19, 20,
   25, 27, 28, 29, 31
spices 28
spores 20, 21
squirting cucumbers 16
stems 8, 9, 11, 18, 20, 26
strawberries 18
sundews 13
sycamores 16

T

thorns 22
toadstools 20
trees 4, 6, 7, 8, 14,
   17, 18, 19, 22,
   24, 25, 30, 31

V

vegans 29
Venus flytraps 12

W

water lilies 10
water plants 4,
   10–11